Umbrellas in the SKY!

THE MALL

Written by
Gloria Jackson

Print information available on the last page

Rev. date: 02/22/2016

To order additional copies of this book, contact:
Xlibris
1-888-795-4274
www.Xlibris.com
Orders@Xlibris.com

Umbrellas
in the
Sky!

Written by
Gloria Jackson

Umbrella's In the Sky!
Umbrella one (1)
Loves jumping on the sun
She enjoys the beautiful light
It's so much fun!
Umbrella two (2)
Enjoys sitting on the moon
Eating his favorite chocolate ice cream
With his big moon spoon!
Umbrella three (3)
Has her own personal tree
A tree in the sky
Right where she wants to be!
Umbrella four (4)

He loves dancing with the stars
They are bright as they can be
They shine from afar!
Umbrella five (5)
She keeps the love alive
She'll make you feel happy
When you're down inside!
Umbrella six (6)
He's from the dark pit
He tries to steal happiness
From all the ones who's lit
Up by the bright light
That shines from above
The kind of light that's special

It's called the light of love!
The most high is wise
He gives us love, protection
And peace
To all the ones who's living
Down to the deceased!
Umbrella seven (7)
She lives in Heaven
Along with nine (9)
Ten (10) and eleven (11)!
Umbrella eight (8)
He's always late
His mind is confused
Between love and hate!

Umbrella nine (9)
She, let's her light shine
She's always dancing
Leaving no one behind!
Umbrella ten (10)
He's always up to win
Little known prince
Loves playing the violin!
Umbrella eleven (11)
Enjoys sitting on the cloud
Doing great things
To make his father proud!
Umbrella twelve (12)
Watch out, she does spells

She's a very wicked woman
Who gathers up souls to sell!
Umbrella thirteen (13)
He's a mighty fine king
He lives on the rainbow
Right beside his future queen!
Umbrella fourteen (14)
Loves to twirl and sing
She lives on the cloud of rain
Beside 13, her future king!
Umbrella fifteen (15)
He can get a little mean
When things, gets dirty
Then he screams

Pick it up,
Get it right
And I don't care
If it takes all night!
Umbrella sixteen (16)
She plays with thunder
So, keep God close
So, she won't tear you asunder!
Umbrella seventeen (17)
He's lightning blue
He'll strike his lights whenever
So getting a clue is on you!
All the umbrellas has to come together
Under one (1) roof

No one (1) can hide
Up high is proof!
Day one (1)
Wasn't fun
Umbrella one (1)
Didn't have her sun!
Day two (2) is blue for umbrella two (2)
He needs his moon
To get back into his happy mood!
Day three (3) Day three (3)
Is cold as can be
The bad umbrellas
Did a lot of bad things!
Day four (4)

Is more horror
The bad umbrellas
Has more in store!
They filled up buckets
And hung them high
They want to make the good miserable
And see them cry!
The good umbrellas are playing
Having a lot of fun
Then here comes the mud out of the buckets
Getting them all one (1) by one (1)!
The good umbrellas starts crying
And running off the floor
Crying out, why did they do this?

What did they do this for?
Day five (5)
Is a different day
The good umbrellas are not letting anything
Stand in their way!
They started singing and dancing
And twirling in the sun
Six (6) and twelve (12)
Are jealous
Because, they want in on the fun!
Day six (6)
Is a trip
Six (6) and twelve (12)
Both flipped!
Because, the others came together
And changed up the weather
But, six (6) and twelve (12)

Told them that darkness is better!
All the others, starts laughing
They said, you both will see
That the light is better
And darkness destroys dreams!
Darkness can and will
Give you a lot of things
But, in return you'll get a cell
For all eternity!
Hot flames
Burning brains
Your entire body
Locked down with chains!
All are being tortured
Over and over again
Screaming for forgiveness
Until, the very end!
Day seven (7)
Is finally here
And the mission is complete
All the good umbrellas went high
To get their favorite treats!
They are jumping and dancing
To their favorite beats
And eating everything
They can possibly eat!
Six (6) and twelve (12)

Went to their burning cell
Trying to figure out
A way for them to bail!
So, do you prefer, the darkness
Or, do you want the light
Darkness is wrong
And the light is right!
If you want to go high
Then, keep God, and pray
His powers are so magnificent
He defeats evil every day!

Printed in the United States
By Bookmasters